MIND
BODY
MASTERY

MIND BODY MASTERY

How to Transform your Life from Reasons to Results

by
MELISSA MAHER

© 2016 by Melissa Maher

Better Days Now

All rights reserved. This book or any portion thereof may not be reproduced or used in any manner whatsoever without the express written permission of the author except for the use of brief quotations in a book review.

Although the author and publisher have made every effort to ensure that the information in this book was correct at press time, this book is not intended as a substitute for the medical advice of physicians. The reader should regularly consult a physician in matters relating to his/her health and particularly with respect to any symptoms that may require diagnosis or medical attention. While every effort has been made to make the information presented here as complete and accurate as possible, it may contain errors, omissions or information that was accurate as of its publication but subsequently has become outdated by marketplace or industry changes or conditions, new laws or regulations, or other circumstances. Neither author nor publisher accepts any liability or responsibility to any person or entity with respect to any loss or damage alleged to have been caused, directly or indirectly, by the information, ideas, opinions or other content in this book/manual/course. If you do not agree to these terms, you should immediately return this book/manual/course for full refund.

For any information regarding permission contact
Melissa Maher via

WWW.BETTERDAYSNOW.CA

Printed in the United States of America
First publication, 2016.

Paperback ISBN - 978-1-988364-00-1

Book cover design by
Justin Garrafa

Dedication

This book is dedicated to my Queen Makeeba and her cousins; Meagan, Keelin, Saphira, Caitlin and Keaghan. May you always be empowered to live the life of your dreams.

Table of Contents

Foreword ix

Acknowledgements xiii

Introduction 1

Chapter 1: The Good, The Bad, The Ugly 15

Chapter 2: Dazed and Confused 31

Chapter 3: Diamonds on the Inside 47

Chapter 4: Dancing in the Rain 55

Chapter 5: Lean In 69

Chapter 6: Believe in Better Days 75

Chapter 7: You've Got The Power 79

Chapter 8: Creating Heaven on Earth: 55 things to live better days, now! 87

Chapter 9: Self-Awareness is Key! 107

Since the writing of this book… 119

About the Author 123

Foreword

By: Marnie Kay

Mind Body Mastery could mean many things dependent upon your background, education or chosen field of expertise. However, in its simplest form, I believe it to be the connection between our physical, mental, emotional and spiritual forms. The truth of which, can only be experienced in two ways, self-awareness and self-expression. Self-awareness requires us to look inward, while self-expression is putting our thoughts and feelings into action deriving an outcome or result in our lives.

I meet many people all over the world today who's results aren't where they want them to be. Somewhere along the way, the connection between physical, mental, emotional and spiritual breaks down, causing us to feel lost, overwhelmed or stressed out, unloved and ultimately unworthy. So, what happened? Where did we go wrong? And more importantly, what can we do to 'go right'?

In this beautiful book, you will find the answers and the inspiration to these questions.

Like Melissa, many years ago, I found myself in a place in my life I didn't want to be. I was stuck in a job that was sucking the life out of me, enveloped by insurmountable debt, managing lacklustre relationships and, I was physically the unhealthiest I had ever been. How might a bright young woman with all the opportunity in the world end up here you might ask? I asked myself the same question. What I wasn't asking myself was what I could do about it.

This drastic shift in perspective only came about when I opened up to the idea that life could be different, and to the idea that someone else could show me how. I found my inspiration in the books I read and people I began to surround myself with. Without them, I wouldn't be who and where I am today. And in fact, I have learned that such a lifestyle shift can only take place with either of those two things, ideally, the combination of both.

Some of the information and the tools that helped me create a dramatic shift in my life, is in this very book. If you're anything like me- you need a practical guide, some 'how-to' and some ongoing encouragement along the way. But it starts with a decision. A decision that you want change more than you are afraid of it. That you are willing to step out and do something about it and inevitably, get back up when you fall down. With that- you can do anything you set your heart on.

One of my favorite quotes is that of J.K Rowling, from her famous Harvard Commencement Address in 2008 entitled "The Fringe Benefits of Failure and the Importance of Imagination."

"Some failure in life is inevitable. It is impossible to live without failing at something, unless you live so cautiously that you might as well not have lived at all- in which case, you fail by default."

We all fail. We all fall down. We all mess up. It's what we do after that that defines us, that builds strength and courage to keep going and eventually, finally succeed. Show me anyone who has done anything of any importance, and I'll show you someone who has failed many times before the apparent 'success'.

Why is failure important in this story of Mind Body Mastery? Because mastering anything in life requires much practise, obviously some failure and ultimately the development of ourselves, the personal growth required to succeed.

As Melissa says...

"Change is difficult at the beginning, messy in the middle, and glorious on the other side. It all starts with a decision and a belief in ourselves that we can do it."

I have watched Melissa grow into a beautiful, confident, inspiring leader, one who has helped many others create change in their lives applying the very principles you are about to read in this book. I have encouraged her to share her story, her practises in a way that will reach many more people for years to come and believe she has done so, magically, in Mind Body Mastery.

If you are truly looking to create change or transform your life in any area, then I encourage you to immerse yourself in this book. The stories, the lessons and the practical tools in the pages that follow are just words and ideas- it is the action that will make them come alive in your life- taking you to a whole new level of Mind Body Mastery, and from reasons to results!

Marnie Kay
Best-Selling Author & Speaker
Founder & CEO of Meraki House Publishing Inc.
www.marniekay.com
www.merakihousepublishing.com

Acknowledgements

"Alone we can do so little; together we can do so much"
– Helen Keller

There are so many people I would like to acknowledge who, either directly or indirectly, actioned me to become the greatest version of myself, beginning with our Creator, for all things I do, I do through you. I Love You.

Following closely in second, I want to thank and acknowledge myself. Melissa, you rock! I am so proud of you and the woman you are becoming. I am impressed by your strength, courage, determination, and willingness to just "go for it" in life. You are a beacon of the light and I am proud of you.

To my little ones – Meagan, Keelin, Spahira, Keaghan, and Caitlin – you light up my life. I am so proud to be your Auntie. You have taught me how to live, and you have taught me how to love. Everything I do, I do for you and so that you know anything is possible in life. Always remember, Auntie is proud of you and I love you to the moon and back plus forever and a day!!

To my mom - thank you for being my #1 supporter with everything I do, I appreciate and value you. You may not always see my vision, yet you see the drive in me and that is enough for you. Thank You, I love you!

To my dad – it has been a pleasure working with you in editing this book. Your skills in literacy really helped transform this book into something great. Thank you for your support and willingness to be part of this project. I love you.

To my entire family, near and far, blood or connected through our souls – thank you for being with me along this journey we call life, it wouldn't be the same without you. Some of my greatest lessons have come from you. I value all the memories from birthday parties and holidays we have created together and all the lessons we learn from each other. I love you.

To anyone I have ever called a friend – whether we still talk or not, I want you to know, you matter to me. Thank you for blessing my life with the good times and the heartache.

To Marnie Kay – Thank you for guiding me through this book writing process and for creating a safe space to say what I need to say. Thank you for all the hard work that is done behind the scenes and thank you for shining your light to illuminate this world.

To Justin – Thank you so much for creating an amazing cover for this book, we are now forever bonded in life (even though that already happened when you married one of my oldest BFF's lol). You really captured my vision and worked tirelessly until it was achieved in print. Thank you for all your efforts.

To Mel – thank you for all your tough love, open ears and open heart. Every time we talk, I know I am speaking to myself (not only because we share the same name) but because I am forever growing and learning when around you. Thank you for your kindness and accepting me for who I am, flaws and all. I truly value you and I believe in you!!

To Guia – Thank you for opening the door for me. All your support and teachings is so valuable to me. Thank you for giving me a chance. I appreciate and value all our time together. Keep shining your light.

To Colleen Proctor- Fillectti and the entire Proctor family – Thank you! Your timing in my life has been impeccable. Thank you for believing in me before I believed in myself. And thank you for being the spark that has set my soul on fire. I am grateful for all the experiences I have shared with you, Bob, and Linda. Thank you for doing all that you do.

To Mr. Happy Face - thank you for Better Days. With you, my legacy was named. You helped me develop my gifts and grow so much, I am forever grateful to you. You have been one of my greatest teachers, and I am honoured to be one of yours too. Thank you for sharing your heart with the world – it is a better place with you in it. Always believe in Better Days.

Introduction

"Forget all the reasons it won't work and believe the one reason why it will."
Author Unknown

This is awesome, the first line in my book. Wow! The hard part is now DONE.

Have you felt like you needed to do something in life and in the same moment felt so scared to do it? Maybe it was to quit your job and start a business. Perhaps it is to forgive someone, or even yourself, for the thing you've held onto from your past. Or, maybe it is dedicating the time to sit down and write your book…. Ahh!! Like right now for me.

You see, everyone has a story, a book or two, within them. We have all experienced major life lessons that have taught us things about ourselves that we didn't even know were there. When these experiences come to us they do so for the sole divine purpose of helping us grow and remember who we truly are.

We always have choices in life, even when it may seem we do not. The choice is always ours when it comes to our life and how we respond to the things that come our way. We can say "Why is this happening to me?" OR we can choose to be more empowered and say, "how is this trying to help me?", "What do I need to learn?"

Plain and simple, in life, we can have REASONS, or we can have RESULTS. And the beauty is – You get to choose.

Now, I have had many reason in life why I wasn't winning. From childhood it started with: Why don't people like me? Why do I have this ugly red hair? Why am I overweight? The reasons continued to grow to include: Why did I get fired? Why did he cheat on me? Why I am always broke? Why am I just not good enough?

WHY WHY WHY WHY... all the WHY's sound like a crying baby for Pete's sake.

I was stuck and couldn't figure out why. Have you ever felt like this? If so, I assure you that you are not alone. Then things began to change. I slowly started to see myself in a slightly different light, and like magic, different results started showing up for me and things started to move in more favourable directions. I didn't care as much to what others thought of me, I cared what I thought of me. I began to love my beautiful red hair, realizing how special and unique it is, not just something that makes me stand out because I look different than others.

I started to discover my personal power and self-worth. Something I never really knew existed. I wasn't entirely sure where all this came from or why things started to change, all I knew was not to stop now.

In 2012, my views on learning and education did a complete turnaround for me. You see, growing up I hated school, I barely got 50%'s and 60%'s. I was never engaged in learning, I didn't have the drive for it. Then I discovered the world of human potential, an industry I didn't even know existed. Ok, so I knew we had the self-help aisle at the book store, but there is a whole industry behind our own personal development??? I was like a kid in a candy store. Who knew!!

This all came to my awareness when I met one of my most powerful teachers in my adult life, Mr. Bob Proctor. Equipped with my new mentor and fresh view on real education, I was thriving. I began to work and study with Bob because he has clearly mastered the game and has been teaching these concepts for over 50 years.

Bob Proctor is a legend in the field of Human Potential. He has written many books teaching the principles he has applied to his life and business that has yielded him tremendous results, earning him millions of dollars, and being able to build schools in Africa with that money too. This man taught me all about the power of the unconscious mind and the immutable laws of the universe. I could write at least ten books about all the learnings and personal insight gained from applying these teachings in my life.

One of the laws he teaches is the law of Cause and Effect – every action has a reaction. This one principle has really allowed me to step into my own personal power, stop making excuses, and get the results I want in my life. Wouldn't it be great to unleash your limitless potential utilizing universal laws, rediscover things about yourself you deleted a long time ago from your memory, and kick all your reasons to the curb? If you answered yes to any of these questions, this book is made specifically for you.

Throughout this book will be woven in some of the powerful learnings and insights I have attained, and I am so thrilled to share with you. This book will allow you to wrap your hands around how you can always stay in control of your life. You will be able to speak your truth with confidence and be able to see the experiences life brings you as opportunities to grow and learn more about yourself and your strengths. You will be equipped with tools to help shift your mindset into a more positive one, one that knows life isn't happening *to* you, it is happening *for* you and your excellence.

Reading this book, you are going to learn how you always have choices in life. You will learn how true and lasting transformation occurs when we align ourselves mentally, emotionally, physically, and spirituality. You will learn some of the world's TOP mind / body techniques that I use to guide my clients in getting the results they desire.

Finally, you are going to gain a deeper understand of how truly powerful your mind is and how living at cause in life will give back your power. There will be no more room for excuses or reasons why things can't get done in life, there will only be room for major self-awareness and massive results.

I'd imagine you may be wondering, why me? Well, it's good to wonder, isn't it? First of all, I've been there and have stayed there way to long. Once I started to wake up and realize how much potential we truly have, I got obsessed with the desire of learning more and tapping into our limitless human potential. I began to study the greats, learned for myself, applied and got the results and now I teach and share this with others.

My background is in communications and the study of human potential. I am a Master Practitioner of Neuro-Linguistic Programming (NLP) and Certified Hypnotherapist graduating second in my class last year (WOOHOO). All this looks great on paper, and yet the real reason why you should consider what I have to say has nothing to do with what I just listed and everything to do with what I have experienced and grown from. All the stories that I was spinning around in caused a really BIG mess in my life and I was able to ditch that s*** once and for all.

One day, it came out of nowhere, I made a decision to stop the crap, take the pen and write the happily ever after to my life. Plain and simple, I turned my MESS into my MESSAGE, and I invite you to do the same too. I will help you. Now, let's make one thing clear upfront. As my trainer Gina Mollicone-Long would always say, "Don't believe a word I say." And I mean that. My truth does not need to be your truth. Take the principles and teachings in this book and formulate your own truth from it. Never assume anything as your own truth, unless it is. Question everything. Research and discover for yourself what resonates with you and what doesn't. Define your own truths in life.

I wonder if you would like to join me on this journey for a while? A journey that has glimpses into the creation, evolution, and manifestation of this book. Let us begin...

This book began as I was working a night shift in late 2013. I was sitting in the Canadian Room at the Royal York hotel, one of the big fancy rooms that hosts gala, conferences etc. Pen in hand, I started to lay out the frame work. What did I want to talk about, what did I have to share? I got a few chapters planned out and then the notebook went on a shelf and was untouched for a few years. I thought to myself "Who am I to write a book?" Clearly, I didn't believe in myself... yet. I worked some pretty cool jobs in my day (security at the Air Canada Center and Royal York Hotel.) I know, laugh it out if you must. I loved that the job was cool and different each day, yet I was super unfulfilled and seeking a way out.

I found it, but it was a slow progression to transition from working for someone else to building my business full time. I attended a book writing seminar and was all inspired. I took the formula, got a nice new note pad and started to get to work. I would brainstorm, create chapter titles, and prepare a layout of what I wanted to write about. I was ready to go yet didn't (typical of me at the time – really good at starting things, awful at completing them).

Now fast forward to September 2015. I am at an event with my good friend, and now publisher, Marnie Kay. We were both on a panel for a women's empowerment talk. She was doing her thing, sharing her story, then suddenly, I had an **Epiphany**, the clouds in the heavens parted and I was ready to take action. When she sat back down beside me I said it out loud "I am going to write my book". Like the awesome Aussie she is she replied with "Ok Mate, let's set a date." That was it. I was no longer carrying the notebook and pen around, I was actually doing it. And here I am now.

One Skype call later with her listening, and I talking, allowed a clear message to formulate, chapter ideas were laid out and deadlines set. This woman has such a gift, it is truly amazing how she pulled it all together for me. My original title for this book was "The untold truths behind a beautiful smile". It really had deep meaning for me because throughout my life, I discovered the most beautiful smiles often carry the deepest pains. For those of you who know me, you know my smile. You have seen me on the brightest day and on the darkest day with the same smile. On the bright days, it would light up an entire city. On the darkest of days, it lacked sparkle. Yet no matter what, you would always see me smile.

And this I know for sure: a smile can heal, a smile can be heard, and a smile can be the only good thing that happens in someone's day. A smile is a gift for you to give and for you to receive.

Another session with Marnie and we decided on another title: A Million Reasons Why: How to transform your life from Reasons to Results. It plays on two folds and I'll explain why. I used to have a million and one reasons why life sucked, why I wasn't good enough, why bad things always happened to me. You name it that was me. I was a great "story-teller" and I was so unconscious to it all. Then one day my million reasons why turned into one powerful WHY. I finally attained that one reason, because that's all you ever need, and all the million reasons disappear into the darkness of the night and finally my light was bright again. So, we moved forward. I loved it, she loved it, and we were rolling.

Then, in the middle of the night in late January, my unconscious mind woke me up to let me know I needed to change my title to Mind Body Mastery: How to Transform Your Life from Reasons to Results. It felt so right. I was running my 8-week program called Mind Body Mastery and the fit was so right. It has become my truth and I knew it was perfect. Ok, enough of the background stuff, let's get right into it now.

Below is one of my first key teachings I learned from Bob Proctor. If you have ever heard him speak or study any of his programs you are probably familiar with the world famous "Stick Person". Well, ok it is only world famous in my world lol. Nonetheless, this one concept completely changed my understanding of the mind, and Bob often shares how this is one of the most powerful things he has learned too.

You see, our unconscious mind works with images and symbols. Have you ever wondered "Where is the mind?" "What does it look like?" well many have, and without being able to provide a specific answer, these questions will cause confusion. A confused mind will only create more chaos. Ray Standford taught this to Bob Proctor many years ago and Bob now teaches this to as many people as he can. Visit www.proctorgallagherinsstitue.com to learn more and view the image of the Stick Person.

Often someone will associate an image of the brain and call it the mind. That is not the case. The mind is in all things, your fingernails, your hair and your pores. The brain is a receiving station to direct the body to do what your mind is asking it to do, yet it is not the mind.

The conscious mind is our thinking mind. It can accept or reject any idea you give it. Our conscious mind entertains new ideas. We have been taught to perceive the world through our five sense which are: sound, sight, smell, taste and touch yet we have higher faculties available to us that are not taught in school. They include: Imagination, Intuition, Memory, Will, and Perception.

The unconscious (or subconscious mind) is our feeling mind as it works with emotions. The beauty about the wonderful unconscious mind is that it cannot distinguish between what's real and what's not, and we can use this to our benefit. Say for example you are looking to increase your income for a year. When you impress upon the unconscious mind the belief and emotion that you have already attained this goal, when you act as if it is already happening, the unconscious mind cannot distinguish what's real and what's not, so it will work with those vibrational frequencies and draw them more into your conscious awareness.

Our unconscious mind also stores all behavior, all learnings and all change. Our unconscious mind gets emotionally involved with the idea causing the body to take action in the direction that supports the attainment of your desires. Wouldn't you agree, this is just amazing?

What else is available to us that we have never been aware of before? I love the saying "You Don't Know What You Don't Know." Keep that statement in mind as you read through the following pages and my hope is you discover something new in this book.

Now, before we continue and get any deeper into this book, I want to make one thing crystal clear. **Change is uncomfortable**, period, no ifs, and's, or buts about it. Wouldn't you agree being stuck in life is uncomfortable too? Which would you prefer? If you are willing to be uncomfortable temporarily, you will be sure to bear the fruits of that discomfort. If you choose to stay the same, that is ok too. Just know that we get what we give in life. No matter how many times you mess up, if you are willing to take responsibility for your life, those mistakes can be turned into something great – if you so choose. Push yourself through the discomfort – Greatness is within you and sunshine awaits you on the other side of your fears.

Throughout the following chapters I welcome you into my world with love and grace. I welcome you to find yourself in me. I acknowledge that I am perfectly imperfect, and I encourage you to take the lessons seriously so you can begin to move in the direction of your dreams, even if you do not know what they are just yet.

I invite you to play full on. Anything less than 100% in life is self-sabotage. Do yourself the favor, play to win! When you are done reading this book you will have a profound sense of self-awareness – what's working for you in life, and what's not. You will have experienced multiple shifts in perception that will aid you in developing your own personal power and teach others to do the same too.

Some chapters will have an exercise or follow up work to do, do them!! It is through application and action that all our desires come to us. We can think and dream all we want, and if we avoid taking action – it means nothing to our future.

I will teach you through my own life experiences and knowledge I acquired how all the great thought leaders of the world consistently get results. How you too can drop the bullshit and grab a hold on your life once again. So, get ready, curl up and let's begin this ride.

CHAPTER 1

The Good, The Bad, The Ugly

"Faith and Fear both demand you to believe in something you cannot see. You choose!"
Bob Proctor

Growing up the middle child in a Catholic family had many challenges for a girl like me. From a young age I never felt like I fit in, I always felt different. I was an energetic child who was HIGHLY self-conscious about the way I looked and what people thought of me. Most of my time was consumed and brainwashed; comparing myself to the standards society put on me as a girl to look a certain way, to have certain things; and frankly, I wasn't measuring up... at all.

I constantly had a longing for external validation and love. I loved everybody and everything. Pet's, friends, you name it, I loved. From a young age, I would have bridal magazines and daydream about my perfect prince charming (thanks Disney for messing us all up with that one lol), never realizing it was me I had to love first.

All the cliché and cheesy sayings were all proven to be true. "If you do not love yourself, no one else will" or "You teach people how to treat you" or the classic question of "How can you truly love someone if you cannot love yourself first?" It has taken a while and now the illusion is being uncovered by many people that *all things we need reside within*. So many young people, and adults too, struggle with wrapping their minds around this simple fact. *You have everything you need and it's all up to you.* Will you push yourself outside of your comfort zone to get something you want? Wouldn't you agree that in order to get something you never had, you're going to have to do something you have never done? Makes sense, right? So, why wouldn't you just go for it in life? What's holding you back? What are you choosing to do, or not do, that is causing you to stay stuck in that boring comfort zone of yours? Let's face it, we also know that life begins at the end of your comfort zone, so go get uncomfortable as this is where you will grow.

It is a big reason and motivation of why I work even harder for people just like you. People who know there is more than this to life are living. I will say that statement again. **All that you need resides within.** There is no lack, there is only abundance. There is no fear, there is only love. There is no separation, there is only oneness. We can live in complete peace and harmony within ourselves when we make choices that serve us and our highest good. The flood gates of abundance and love will open and pour right in like magic when you have your reasons.

I was a chubby kid who was completely detached from my body, hating every aspect of it. Not knowing this was my vehicle to navigate through this lifetime. I did everything possible to hide my true feelings so that the outside world wouldn't know I hated myself and felt very depressed. Little did I know, every thought and emotion manifests itself in physical form, and boy was my body showing its form! In this book, I will teach you how to utilize your body to master your state of mind, how to know if a thought or decision is right for you, and how to pay attention in the moment now.

My model of the world was one of feeling alone. I felt

alone in my family, having an older sister who always got to do everything first, and a younger brother who just got babied and given everything he wanted too – typical middle child syndrome, I know. I wasn't very close with my family growing up. We never really sat down and had open conversations, get to know each other etc. It was like 5 people, and a couple of pets, co-habituating in the same house.

Physically, I would constantly feel sick and tired. I went through a phase of starving myself and making myself throw up in hopes of losing weight. When that didn't work, I would binge eat and gain pounds and pounds seemly overnight. I even abused alcohol in my teen years. I had no respect or love for myself, which I identified as only my body. I contemplated suicide and thought if I were to take enough pills this could just end now, the pain was so much at times. I would always be crying and wanting to die.

As I got into my teen years things got worse. I became more self-conscious and harmful to my body. I can recall on a couple of occasions an awakening happening. I remember looking at myself in the mirror, catching a glimpse deep into my eyes and having a profound connection. I would then look at my face and in turn my body and have a sense of awareness inside me that I am not this image. I am looking in the mirror (aka my body) and I AM that what I was looking at in my eyes. Little did I know then that I was discovering that I, she who calls herself Melissa Maher, is not this physical body, but the soul living within this body. It took me well into my 20's to believe this. This was a beginning for me.

Years ago, when I began my studies of the mind body connection, I came across a life changing book by author Louise Hay – it is called "You Can Heal Your Life". This book helped me realize how much of our mental and emotional beings are reflected in our physical bodies. As mentioned in the previous chapter, the law of cause and effect, for every action there must be a reaction. Well, little did I know, all my self-hatred was showing up in my physical body, in the fat or bad skin or alcohol abuse.

In my younger years, I constantly felt like I never measured up. I hated being different for having red hair. There wasn't many of us, and despite having adults tell me I have gorgeous hair, I was picked on and made fun of by my peers. It just wasn't the same. I remember wanting to dye my hair just so other would like and accept me. I told myself all kinds of stories as to why people didn't like me, and you couldn't tell me they weren't true.

Have you ever felt this way? Have you heard yourself say something so inaccurate and false about yourself that was based simply on opinions and not facts? Have you ever seen yourself in a light that simply was not true? If so, I can relate with you.

Now stay with me on this one...

When we have REASONS in life we are making up stories that are simply not true. "Oh, I won't like that food, I do not want to try it." This is something I still do today. And I challenge you (and myself as well), how do you know you will not like it if you do not try it? That is a lame story you are telling yourself.

Part of my job working with clients is to stop you from running the stories you use and move you into an area of possibilities. You see, living in possibilities is so much more fun and exhilarating. Here we can use our imagination and get creative in the ways our desired outcomes will come through.

REASONS are just stories, and remember, you can have REASONS, or you can have RESULTS – not both! The choice is always yours.

One of the hardest parts is kicking the stories to the curb, and it is also one of the most beautiful parts too. I found that when we are living at cause, we get to make up whatever ending we want. We are in control of how that story will unfold, and even if it doesn't end the way we wanted it to, we can still be happy and grateful for what we receive as we know it was all meant to be.

Eventually, I unconsciously started to unravel all the bullshit stories I would tell myself. I began to do that which I wanted to do – like play soccer just for the fun of it, not because I must be any good at it. I also started to realize that by surrounding yourself with the ones who make you feel safe, to be who you are is essential. I am blessed to have had people in my life who made me feel that way. My dear childhood friends Frevi and Shellie. These two girls loved me for myself. Accepted me for myself, and to this day, still remind me of how awesome I am and can be. I have known these two since grade 1 and we still keep in touch today – I am so grateful and love you!

As mentioned in the intro, when I first decide to write this book the title was going to be "The untold truths behind a beautiful smile". This title spoke volumes to me and many people I shared it with. I would invite you to keep this in mind in the following chapters and I will explain why.

Many people who suffer from depression do not appear this way on the outside. I was one of those people. If you ever suffered from depression, I am willing to bet that at one point or another you did not appear that way on the outside. Depression is a silent killer. Many people suffer in silence, never telling anyone what goes on inside themselves or behind closed doors. For me, there were many nights of crying myself to sleep. Many days of staying in bed not being able to get out. Many months of extreme exhaustion, whether due to a sleepless night, or sleeping all day. I would go out into the world as bright and as beautiful as can be, smiling and laughing, and in those moments, feeling good. Then, almost out of nowhere, I would be driving (my car was a big cry fest for me) or I would step foot into my home and just burst out into tears. I had no idea why. I would just cry, feel worthless and sorry for myself, and then when all that was done, I would berate myself for feeling that way. I would yell at myself to snap out of it – Why are you so happy other times and not now – what is wrong with you I would ask.

The truth is, there were many truths I did not speak. Many people reading this book will be shocked and surprised because they know me as the happy, positive, bubbly Melissa. They will be in disbelief that these statements are true. If you have ever suffered from depression, you know what I mean ... you will know this to be true.

My depression taught me many things about myself and other people. It taught me to always treat people with love and respect, you never know what they are going through. It taught me that feeling sad is ok, staying sad is not. It is actually healthy to feel all emotions. If you were to only feel happy all the time, I would be concerned.

Depression is not something you can just kick to the curb with a simple positive thought process. It requires major shifts in perception, much more than any positive affirmation can provide. You have a choice every day, do I want to live in peace and happiness? Or do I want to live in depression and misery? That statement may be a bit bold for some of you, yet it is very true. Choose in THIS moment to be happy. Not all moments will be that of joy and happiness, however, if you choose right now to be in a positive state, you are ahead of the game.

When I began to understand how powerful the unconscious mind is, I realized that it is my choice. When you can have enough self-awareness in yourself you will see how this applies to you too. Your unconscious mind is so loyal and loves to follow instructions. It also cannot discern between what is real and what is imagined. This is something I now use to my advantage, let me teach you how.

Our unconscious mind cannot distinguish between what's real and what's not. It also cannot process a negative. For example, if I were to say to you right now "Don't think of a blue tree", what happened? You imagined a blue tree, didn't you? That's my point. It supports us with whatever we ask from it. If we say, "My life sucks", "I hate life" "Nobody likes me", our beautiful unconscious mind will give us more situations to prove us right. It gives us what we ask for, whether this is really what we want or not. Be very specific with what you want, and always ensure it is positively stated.

One way you can do this is with goal setting and affirmations. When you "act as if" you already have what it is you desire, your unconscious mind will work to bring that for you stronger. This beautiful part of our brain is called the Reticular Activating System – or RAS. Its sole function is to filter all the things that come into your awareness and bring you more of what you asked it to bring to you. It takes instructions from your conscious mind and passes them onto your unconscious mind.

Have you ever had this happen to you – you are interested in purchasing a new vehicle, you did your research, picked the car and a very special colour you want (which you have never seen on that model before) and started shopping around. Suddenly, you start to see this particular car EVERYWHERE you go? Same colour and all. Well, your RAS has been activated and you notice it more. It is not that those cars were never around before, it is just that you have set your focus onto it, and your RAS is now showing you more examples of it.

This is something so powerful and I encourage you to test it out for yourself. Perhaps tomorrow, set the intention to see as many purple cars as possible. Pick a colour that is not so common and really BELIEVE you will see it. This happened to me one day while testing it out. I said I was going to see one PINK car today. I focused my intention and really believe I was going to see it. I then released this intention to the universe and my beautiful unconscious mind and went about my day. Later in the afternoon, I was driving and drove past a car dealership close to my house that had this pink van predominately displayed for me to see it. I cheered inside and laughed out loud, my experiment worked!!! Later that day, I was driving to my sisters, a place I visit often. As I was turning onto her street I see this PINK Mary Kay Cadillac parked in someone's driveway. HOLY CRAP I thought. I have never seen this car there before. I was so giddy. About 20 minutes later, I was leaving and what drives past me? That same pink Cadillac. Even though I had already seen it once before, I counted it as 3 pink cars that day. This was too much of a "coincidence" that as I was leaving it just happened to drive past me. My belief level raised immensely after this experiment. Do it, it will for you too!

My point of this story is to focus on what you want!!! When you believe that the universe is always working in your favor, life becomes magical.

In order for you to successfully achieve and maintain change in your life there are three important requisites for that change to occur. These three things are required to get the **RESULTS** you want in your life. They are:

1. **Clean up** your past

2. Take **ACTION**

3. **FOCUS** on what you **WANT**

These three things are critical for your success. They may seem small, and they probably are, however, so many people miss these principles and wonder why they do not get the results they want in life. It is usually because they are not focusing on what they want.

Pay attention next time you ask someone what they want in life (or in a partner, job, with the children etc.) They will most likely list all the things they DON'T want, barely mentioning anything that they do want. Ask any of your single friends, what are they looking for in a partner and they will start to say, "I don't want a person who smokes, I don't want someone who is broke, I don't want…." And then the other half of the time, they don't even know what they want. Would you be willing to go on a road trip with me, to New Orleans (somewhere I haven't been yet), with no GPS? Probably not. We wouldn't end up at our destination. We would get lost, waste a lot of time and money on gas and not even enjoy the trip because we would be so worried about finding our way, we wouldn't be able to enjoy the view. Well, life is like that too. We must have clear objectives and goals and a willingness to use the GPS or map if it is not a place we have been before. In life, our mentors and coaches are the maps guiding us to where we want to be.

Below, I invite you to write down some specific things you want in life. Just jot down what comes to mind. Dream BIG and ensure it is stated in the exact way you want it to come true. After this, I invite you to write a positive affirmation about your goal and read it every single day for 30 days. This will really invoke inside of you the burning desire to achieve this goal. Feel the feelings, hear all the sounds, see yourself achieving it. It is a simple task and yet can be very challenging to complete for 30 days. Do It! Give this gift to yourself. Do it with excitement and a full heart.

One of Bob Proctor's favorite affirmations is:

"I am so happy and grateful now that money comes to me in increasing quantities, through multiple sources, on a continuous basis."

I WANT.....

_____

_____

_____

_____

_____

Now take any of the above desires and write out the affirmation below and read it every day for 30 days. Tell me what happens after the 30 days, I would love to hear your experience.

When writing any of your goals, I will give you a simple technique. Write it in the present tense. Act as if you already have it. Remembering the unconscious mind does not know what is real and what is imagined. To put any goal into the present tense, begin with: I am so happy and grateful now that... Another key element is that it has a date of completion. Here is an example of what I mean.

I am so happy and grateful now that I have earned $100,000 or more on or before December 31st, 2016.

Even though this date has yet to come, the goal is still in the present tense and has the deadline, so my unconscious mind now knows exactly what I want. It is up to me to take action on the opportunities that present themselves to me to achieve this goal. Now it is your turn. Take one of the above desires and write out your affirmation to active your RAS below.

I am so happy and grateful now that….

_____

_____

_____

_____

_____

_____

_____

_____

Great work!! Now take this affirmation and read it every day for 30 days!! Get all your senses involved, feel all the feelings you will feel once you have achieved this goal. You can even write out the affirmation for an extra power boost daily if you want to take it a step further. And now go get 'em… the possibilities are endless for you. I am proud of you.

CHAPTER 2

Dazed and Confused

"The one thing you have that nobody else has is you. Your voice, your mind, your story, your vision."
– Neil Gaiman

If you do not have a strong heart and a strong mind, life will chew you up and spit you out. A solid foundation is the key and many people are missing this. It is not the fault of the parents either, it is the faults of us all. When we know better, we do much better. People today need to step up and demonstrate, through actions, what we would like to see in this world. When this is missing, we take all those stories and past mistakes and drag them into our future. That's exactly what happened to me.

As I entered my 20's, I had so many views of the world that were not conducive to my personal growth and I couldn't figure out why I wasn't getting ahead. Most of my friends I grew up with were going away to university, getting married, and were in careers. I on the other hand was just working job's and still trying to find my way into a career path that fulfilled me. All I knew was that I wanted to help people. I took many different programs at local colleges in Toronto, never feeling the passion I feel about the work I do now. I had no money in the bank, very poor relationships, and mental and emotional scars that dug very deep within me. I kept running the same stories over and over of why I wasn't getting ahead in life.

The peak of my depression began around the age of 17 and lasted several years. I was in a relationship that tore me apart and ripped me open in every sense of the word. Little did I know, this would be a critical defining moment in my life. Looking back now, this was the epitome of where I allowed "reasons" to run my life instead of taking ownership and getting results. He was a year older than me and came from a broken home, in and out of the foster care system. I thought I could help him, show him the love he never received before, be the love that would "fix" him.

Most of my life, I sought external validation from people.

I wanted to be accepted and fit in. At times, that meant compromising myself, my values, and my beliefs. All I wanted was to be loved, not realizing that love comes from within, not from other people. This relationship would be my first major lesson in this. How could I love someone if I couldn't even love myself?

We dated for about two years, I don't remember much from the beginning or how long we were "happy" for. It seems irrelevant now. It is only in the darkest of times that we can see our light. Only in time, would I be able to spark my light and set myself on fire. When you allow reasons to run your life, you give your power away. For two years, I gave my power away. Unconsciously I gave him permission to let his anger to the world be released onto me. Why did I do that? Because I did not love and value myself. This tragic love story didn't start as a horror movie, it started with two broken people trying to figure out how to love.

His anger towards me started small. Then it grew and grew some more. It grew so much that it turned violent. I remember when he first started hitting me all the excuses "reasons", I would give as to why it was ok. "Oh, he only punched me in the arm, that's ok, at least it wasn't my face." When he would hit me in the face "Oh at least he didn't make me bleed or scar." It even extended to violence towards other members of my family. I will never forget those times, in my deepest and darkest moments, how it feels to see how your REASONS not only effect your life, but the life of your family as well. Today, I am working very hard rebuilding the trust of those I lost over 10 years ago. I have forgiven myself and I only pray they forgive me too.

When you avoid standing in your power, people will take advantage of you. Not because they are bad or evil, but because we allow this to happen. Personal power is not only mandatory for yourself, it teaches other people how to do it for themselves, and it teaches them how to treat you. The saying "You teach people how to treat you" is absolutely true. When you begin to live on the cause side in life, people automatically begin to value you more.

I imagine you are wondering, what does all this mean? I am often asked this question. It's good to wonder, isn't it? Standing in your power means you set healthily boundaries with people. To say no when you want to say no and to say yes when you want to say yes. This can show up in any area you're in. At the office, if a co-workers asks you to do something; and you already have a million things on the go, think to yourself first:

1.) Am I able?

2.) Am I willing?

3.) What will it cost me in time/ money/ energy? And under what conditions?

Then make your decision based on this criteria. Often, when we avoid taking a moment to pause and ask ourselves these questions, we can make a decision that pushes our boundaries and we say yes to something when we really wanted to say no.

Have you felt that people push your boundaries? Have you ever heard yourself saying "Why do people take advantage of me?" Can you see how this can apply to areas in your life? It is important to have the self-awareness and personal boundaries. People will respect this. They may not like it, but they will respect it.

What are the boundaries that have been pushed or broken for you lately? Who are the people that push your boundaries? You need to correct this and remake those boundaries with these people. Think about it.

Standing in your power also means knowing what you want and go after it. For me, in my 20's, I became a slave to my mind. I had no clue what I wanted in life, besides "be happy", and even if I did know what I wanted, my mindset would not have been conducive to receiving all that I desired. Being happy is not a goal, it is a state. We can be happy in any moment, all you have to do is remember a time when you were. Do it now. Can you remember a time? The choice is always ours.

Mental slavery is plaguing our country, and our world today. We look outside ourselves to see what's "cool". Who should I be? What should I be doing in life? What should I look like? It is a lot of pressure and very confusing for people of any age today. I know because it was for me too.

We idolize people we have never met and told to aspire to be like them, because they have "made it". As young adults we are told to go to school, get good grades, get a job, work 40 years retire and then you can start really living, and living on 40% of your salary, might I add. This is Ludicrous! This is not what life is meant to be.

Life is to be glorious, joyous, and adventurous. Life is

meant to excite and grow us into the person we are meant to be. Just look at people on the subway on a Monday morning. People walk like zombies to work. People wait all week until the weekend, all year until summer vacation, and wait their whole life until retirement. Why not live now? As my mentor Bob Proctor teaches, people don't live their life ... they want to live because of their paradigm. Some don't believe it's even possible, "that's just the way it goes" you may hear them say. BULLSHIT!! It is possible!!! You are God's highest form of creation and anything is possible. You just need to decide that's what you want and do what it takes to make it happen.

There is a wonderful publication called "The Common Denominator of Success" by Albert E.N Gary. I was tasked to read this every day for 30 days. The first time I undertook the task, I was assigned to do it with Colleen, Bob's daughter. Colleen and I would set aside 20 minutes every day for the 30 days and we took turns reading out loud. I would read one page, Colleen would read the other. We alternated each day who started, and we got it done, no matter if we had to wake up early, or do it late at night – it got done!

I received tremendous value out of that task and I have

tasked my clients to do the same too.

Over the days reading this book, different lines would stand out more than others. One of those lines that rang bells in my ears when I read it was:

"The common denominator of success --- the secret of success of every man who has ever been successful --- lies in the fact that he formed the habit of doing things that other people don't like to do." – Albert E.N Grey

What does this mean? Well, they don't like to do whatever it is either!!! Yet they know if they push through the discomfort they will yield the results they desire. This is my point, and my truth to you. If there is something you want in life, go for it!! Avoid being a slave to the mind. Use the mind to your benefit and use it to help you get the results you want in life.

Everything you want is on the other side of your comfort zone. If you can become comfortable being uncomfortable the world is yours!! Ask any successful person and they will agree. This applies to not only the big things in life, but the smaller things as well. It is simply about managing your discomfort as change is uncomfortable. Focus on what you want, take the necessary steps to create the new neurology, the neurology of excellence that will support your growth and create the possibilities for your success.

This makes me think of one of my dear friends and mentor James MacNeil. He once said to me, it is simply about taking the very next step. You do not need to know how to get to the end right now, you just have to be willing to take the next step. Wouldn't you agree this is true? Makes sense, right? Just be willing to take the next step and everything else will fall into place. Remember baby steps, one at a time.

The learning process has become more difficult than necessary because of bad feelings we have when we make mistakes. The bad feelings come from judgments like, "not doing it right," "not good enough," "can never learn this," etc.

Ironically, not doing it right and making mistakes are vital steps in the learning process. Yet, too often our attention goes to trying to avoid the bad feelings, rather than to the learning at hand. Understanding the four stages of learning can become a skill that will help keep the learning process focused on learning, rather than feeling bad about ourselves for not knowing how. Below are the four stages of learning as uncovered by Abraham Maslow:

1. Unconscious Incompetence

"I don't know that I don't know how to do this." This is the stage of blissful ignorance before learning begins.

2. Conscious Incompetence

"I know that I don't know how to do this, yet." This is the most difficult stage, where learning begins, and where the most judgments against self are formed. This is also the stage that most people give up.

3. Conscious Competence

"I know that I know how to do this." This stage of learning is much easier than the second stage, but it is still uncomfortable and self-conscious.

4. Unconscious Competence

"What, you say I did something well?" The final stage of learning a skill is when it has become a natural part of us; we don't have to think about it.

Using the example of learning to drive a car, as a child I first thought that all I needed to do was sit behind the wheel and steer and use the pedals. This was the happy stage of unconscious incompetence.

When I began learning to drive, I realized there was a whole lot more to it, and it became a little daunting. This was the stage of conscious incompetence. There were so many different things to do and think about, literally hundreds of new behaviors to learn.

In this stage I made lots of mistakes, along with judgments against myself for not already knowing how to do it. <u>Releasing judgement</u> can be very helpful here in the second stage because mistakes are integral to the learning process. They're necessary because learning is essentially experimental and experience-based, trial and error. Information can be accumulated, but until it is practiced and used, it's only information. It's not learning, and certainly not a skill.

As I practiced, I moved into the third stage of learning, conscious competence. This felt a lot better, but still I wasn't very smooth or fluid in my driving. I often had to think about what to do next, and that felt awkward and uncomfortable.

Finally, after enough practice, I got to the place where I didn't have to think about every little thing I was doing while driving. I thought about my driving only when something alerted me to it. I became unconsciously competent. Because of the ease and grace in unconscious competence, my driving became much safer.

Now understanding the four stages of learning, can you think of a time you gave up on something too soon? Can you bring to mind a moment that failure struck and you decided not to try again? Without judgement, and acknowledging that perhaps you did not have the tools or resources as you do now, what could you have done differently, and are you willing to try it again? When you master your mind, you will be able to see FAILURE as FEEDBACK and not as defeat.

A small shift in perception is all that is required to open yourself up to new possibilities and a new way of life. This one was the one for me. Today, I celebrate failure, I welcome failure and that may sound crazy to some, yet for me, this is part of my truth now. The more you fail, the more you grow. The more you persist in the face of failure, the stronger you become. This is what separates successful people from non-successful people and it applies to ALL areas of life. So say it with me…. **FAILURE** is **FEEDBACK** and failure makes a better ME!!!

Look, let's get real... if we continue to choose to live at effect in life, where everything happens to us and nothing goes our way, I can promise you this... you are wasting your gifts. You are not meant to play small in life. You are meant to shine bright and share that light with other people. The choice is always yours. I invite you to ask yourself... what would my life look like if I did all the things I was too afraid to do right now? What would my life look like if I eliminated the words "I can't" or "Impossible" from my vocabulary? **Side Note:** the word impossible is actually "**I'm Possible**"!! Hello!!! We have had so many smoke and mirrors thrown in our face and we never questioned a single one up until now. I told you at the beginning of this book: question everything!! Formulate your own opinions and make your own truths instead of taking the opinions of others and defaulting them as your own.

Below, or on a separate sheet, I invite you to list a few things that you did that you thought you could never do before doing it. For me, it was doing the CN Tower stair climb and coming in under my goal time. This was a great accomplishment in that I thought it would be more difficult than it was. Now, believe me when I say, it was bloody hard climbing over 1,800 steps, yet I did it in only

27minutes and 31seconds. My goal was 35 minutes!!! I am so proud of myself and I still have the time card from the climb. What was it for you? Perhaps it was giving a presentation in front of a group of strangers? Maybe it was becoming a parent? Or it may even be committing and going to the gym twice a week. Think and dig deep. List below anything you have accomplished, big or small, that before it was done you didn't think it was even possible.

I accomplished the following believing it to be bigger than me:

_____

_____

_____

_____

_____

_____

_____

_____

_____

Looking at this list above, I will invite you to take a few moments to go back to those beautifully empowered times and recall how good it felt to accomplish it. Feel all the positive feelings, hear all the beautiful sounds and see all the beautiful things that happened in order to support you in achieving this. Anchor this feeling right now. Tell yourself, out loud, that you are proud of yourself!!! Say it like you mean it. I am proud of you. (Insert high five here) WOOHOO!!

CHAPTER 3

Diamonds on the Inside

"By being yourself, you put something beautiful into the world that wasn't there before."
Edwin Elliot

Change is difficult at the beginning, messy in the middle, and glorious on the other side. It all starts with a decision and a belief in ourselves that we can do it. Now, let me make one thing clear before I proceed with this chapter... If you want things to change in your life you are going to have to change things in your life. Period. End of story. (Drops the mic).

We cannot use the same thought process that created the current problem and expect it to help us solve it. This is what most people do over and over again and wonder why they are not winning. Albert Einstein said it best: "The definition of insanity is doing the same thing over and over expecting a different result." I can hear the light bulbs going off in your head.

We cannot use the same thinking and habits that caused us to become overweight in the process of releasing it. We cannot follow the budget we never made expecting to create financial freedom. We cannot repair broken relationship with the same blame and hatred that created them. It won't work. And now, I'd imagine everything is starting to become much clearer, wouldn't you agree? This is huge! It definitively was for me.

Where this learning stood out the most for me was in the physical challenges I experienced with my body image. Remember previously I mentioned how so many of us seek external validation and believe the lies we are told that being a size 0 is the only way to be called beautiful? Ya that was me. I constantly felt I wasn't good enough because I couldn't measure up to what society told me to be. I am here to tell you F*@% that!!! You are beautiful just the way you are. That being said, I also acknowledge that I could improve my confidence and sense of self by improving my physical health. Why? Because our outside world is a reflection of our inside world. I started to wrap my mind around that we are more than these physical bodies, yet it was all interconnected. I can look back and see, based on my physical body, when I was the happiest and when I was not. My body always reflected my emotions and mental state of mind. This applies to everyone.

Just before my 30th birthday I woke up and realized my life isn't where I imagined it to be when I was growing up. There is something funny or weird about birthdays that end with a 0 or a 5 that results in us having wake up calls. I realized I was at my highest weight ever, just shy of 200 pounds. I was broke working a dead-end job that really didn't fulfill me, and everything around me just wasn't the way I wanted it.

Then, out of "nowhere" I am online, and I see a post from my sister stating she is selling 30 personal training sessions at a local gym for $1500. I was not in any motivated mindset to commit to anything like that, yet by the grace of God I started typing... "I want them." You see, my sister is someone I silently looked up to my whole life. Growing up, we would argue and fight because I would steal her stuff or just bother her. As we got older, I really saw her become an amazing woman and mom. Between all her pregnancies she worked really hard and released nearly 100 pounds. In that moment when I started typing, I knew that if she could do it, I could do it too. I worked out a payment plan to pay for the sessions with my sister and next thing I knew, I found myself in the gym waiting to meet this person who was going to be my trainer and help me reclaim not only my body, but my whole life.

Never could I have imagined how blessed I was to have this young man named Alvin. He couldn't have been much older than 21 at the time, a baby in my eyes, yet I felt safe and confident he could help me. After the 30 sessions, Alvin helped me realize a side of me that I forgot, or perhaps didn't even know was there. He showed me how I can do anything…. One of his favorite sayings was "You got this. True story lol". It makes me smile even to write it now. I invested a lot of money to work with him and over the course of one year I was able to release nearly 50 pounds with his training and support. Something I am so proud of still to this day. At times in life, all we need is to have someone who believes in us just a tiny bit more than we believe in ourselves, Alvin was that guy for me. He has since gone on to become a professional body builder with his twin brother Terrance, and I am so proud to see him go after his dreams in life.

I was willing to do what I was not comfortable during

that one year. I pushed myself physically AND mentally to achieve those results. There were times I wanted to call in sick, yet I knew I would let him down (and he would work me harder next visit) so I made sure to be there, on time and ready to work. Life works the same way. If you can have someone hold you accountable, teach and guide you, hold space and seeing only your greatness, you too can achieve all the things you desire. When we feel good with ourselves, our life beings to reflect this.

Now, those 50 pounds I released more than half I have put back. Why you may ask? Because I still didn't change my internal view of who I was. I was still the chubby fat kid inside that was running the show. This book for me is all about being open and honest and sharing my true self with you. I want you to wrap your hands around the fact that I know what you are going through too. I'd imagine you're beginning to hear yourself more and more in me and are starting to see all the possibilities that are available to you, just as they are for me.

Those 50 pounds crept back in because I didn't change my mindset around it. Yes, I was proud, yes, I felt good yet there was something missing to really lock in the change for good, and it was my mindset.

Another thing I was saying was I "lost" 50 pounds. Did you notice above I did not say that? I said RELEASED 50 pounds instead. Our language is so important and if we are not conscious of it, it will sabotage us along the way. If you say you want to lose weight, guess what, you might find it again. I sure did. Instead, challenge yourself to state it positively. Say "I live in a healthy body" or "I permanently removed the excess weight in my body". This will make a world of a difference to your unconscious mind.

My studies in NLP has really taught me how our language and self-talk is so vitally important. NLP stands for Neuro Linguistic Programming. Become mindful of your language and self-talk because it creates our reality (remember the unconscious mind does not know what's real or imagined and takes all things literally).

In a moment, I will invite you to think of some negative self-talk or language you use to describe yourself. Find the positivity in the statement (or the opposite of it) and install it using the following technique.

This technique I use several times a day. When you catch yourself having negative thoughts or images in your mind, the goal is to notice it, discard it and replace it with a positive thought, as soon as possible. Say for example it a limiting belief that you don't look good in jeans. You catch the thought when it comes in. Pause. Acknowledge the thought for what it is, just a limiting belief. Then take that limiting belief about yourself (I don't look good in jeans) and visualize throwing it to the sun and burning it. Watch it disintegrate and crumble to ash. Then, take the opposite of the old belief (I look fantastic in jeans), and with a giant sling shot, fire that thought into both your conscious and unconscious mind, replacing the old thought with the new and productive one. Makes sense? Good. Do it now.

CHAPTER 4

Dancing in the Rain

"Light is to Darkness what Love is to Fear: in the presence of one, the other disappears"
Marianna Williamson

What does it feel like to be totally disconnected? To me, it feels like a cold, damp rainy day. The rain makes you want to stay indoors, in bed, out of sight from everyone. How is it that the same day can become sunny, glorious, and warm as well? It is all a matter of perception. Despite a rainy day being a rainy day – why not look at it as a day where the grass is getting watered, or a giant playground for adults and kids to enjoy? Have you ever gone dancing in the rain? I have a couple of times and let me tell you, it is the most childlike and liberating thing ever!!

Can you imagine, and just see yourself for a moment getting rain boots on and going outside and splashing in puddles? Leaning your head back, opening your mouth and drinking the abundance of water that is pouring from the sky? Hear all the rain drops pitter patter on your jacket and listen to the laughter as you jump and splash in the puddles. This is what life is about. This is how we can take a single moment and get connected with our higher selves – try for yourself and go dancing in the rain!

On rainy days it may well be more work to see all the possibilities available to you. It may seem like a bummer because we have to dress in more layers, bring an umbrella and attempt to stay dry. Life is like this when we live disconnected from our higher-self – from our soul. All it takes is a moment in time to see things differently. To choose and shift, moment by moment to reach our greatest and highest good.

"Things are never as bad as they seem." - Harper Lee, To Kill a Mockingbird

Embarking on this journey into self-discovery and self-mastery is a challenging thing. It gets very real and really fast. It is the START that stops most people. The fear of what will be uncovered, what crap will I have to face, and the avoidance of being uncomfortable causes us to live life at effect, remaining stuck in the same place

– the cold, rainy, not so fun place.

Real courage is when you know you're kicked before you begin but begin anyway and see it through no matter what. Allow this to resonate within you.

Discovering the beauty in our pain is the true name of the game. It is all good to speak of love and light and I promise you it is greater than anything out there. I also promise you this, I will not sugar coat any of it. Personal growth into spiritual connection is messy, dark, confusing and lonely. I know because I embarked on my journey a few years ago. In order to grow, we must go into our shadows and learn, release and transcend all that is not love. It is hard work to be open and real, but I promise you the rewards are so incredibility worth it… just like dancing in the rain.

To be totally disconnected spiritually was one of the best things that ever happened to me…. WHAAAAT???!?!?!? You may say??? It was in times like that when I found myself. I discovered I am more than just this physical body, I can be, do and have anything I truly desire knowing it was all planned out eons before I laid foot on this planet.

BREATHE. BELIEVE. BE. This is my recipe.

This book as an example, crazy that I am writing it. Funny thing too, this chapter has caused me to do more "writers block" than any of the other chapters? Why? I am not sure. Perhaps a part of me is shy knowing that now I am in a place of complete and utter vulnerability. You have formulated an opinion about me long before these words were written and if you are still reading this now, thankfully it was probably a good one.

Part of my "disconnect" in life came from always worrying about "what will others think of me". How does that statement make you feel? Can you hear yourself saying the same thing? I sure did. It ran my life for many years. Like me, you may see so many possibilities for your life yet only able to hear the negative self talk in your mind.

> *"People generally see what they look for and hear what they listen for."* **- Harper Lee.**

I'll give you this piece of advice... to quiet the mind is to awaken the soul.

Today, I allow my MESS to be my MESSAGE and this book is an invitation for you to do the same. I am by far the furthest thing from perfection. As I write this, I share with you; my health needs improving, I am working on building a positive net worth, my relationships are improving and yet my faith in the universe has never been stronger.

I know for a fact, everything I do has been pre-planned for me in a world that supports all my wishes and dreams. It is our birthright to live abundantly. There is no lack in the universe, there is only lack in our minds. When we tap into and become connected with the universal life force energy that supports us all equally; is when the real magic begins.

Trusting the process of life can lead to a roller coaster of emotions. And it is all by choice. Self-awareness allows these choices and the process to be evaluated in a different way. When you become more self-aware you can see all the possibilities, the learnings and opportunities are right in front of you. Get curious with life, it is one of the greatest gifts there is.

Self-awareness allowed me to get connected on a deeper level with ME. I became more and more aware of that beautiful light inside of me, and this lead to my ability to connect back with who I truly am – a beacon of the light. More and more these days I have clients show up just like me, am I surprised? No, absolutely not. I have transformed my major disconnect in life into this book. I have transformed it into my business **Better Days Now**. I even transform it into simple conversations that leave a lasting impact. This is what I mean by your mess is your message. You have something inside of you that needs to be shared because you have no idea who it will help. In my opinion, it is selfish of you not to share your message with others – people need to hear you right now.

Self-awareness and your "connection" can show up in many ways. One example I experienced and often point out to others is little "coincidences" or synchronicities. First of all, there are no such thing as coincidences in life. Period. Everything is Divinely timed to be of service to you in that one moment. For example, have you ever thought to do something, and you looked at the clock and it was 11:11 or 2:22 or a series of numbers? These are signs you are on the right path, you are being given encouragement from the spirit world. If you want to dig deeper, why not Google "sacred numbers" or "angel numbers" and see what pieces you can put together to really feel what the message is deep in your core.

Trusting is a skill. Skills are developed over time with repetition and faith. In a previous chapter I outlined the four stages of learning, well it is just like that when it comes to trusting the process of life.

When adversity strikes us, there are many things that go through us and we all deal with it differently. If you haven't wrapped your hands around it by now, this book is really all about how you chose to respond to the things that happen for your own personal growth. Nothing happens TO you, it is all for you to reach your greatest and highest good. It is all in how you see it.

A change in view within can make you more effective and perhaps launch a new element on how you serve in the world. Taking things to the personal level first, rather than being angry at the upside-down world, gives you spiritually-grounded power!

One of the greatest things I have learned in my 33 plus years in this lifetime is that we are not just these physical bodies walking around on this planet living day by day waiting to die. We are WAY more than this. We are spiritual beings, gifted with an intellect, having human experiences. Let me say that again, I want you to really feeeeeel the words here: We are spiritual beings, gifted with an intellect, having human experiences. We are here to learn which is required for our soul's evolution and all the experiences we have in our lives are created for that divine purpose. Therefore, nothing happens to you, everything is happening for you.

A couple of years ago I was inspired to experience a Reiki session. The word kept coming into my awareness, I would hear people talk about it, see a post or two online about it and one day I decide to find someone to share it with me. It was exhilarating!! I really enjoyed it. I had another friend suggest I should consider learning more about it and become attuned to it because when you give Reiki, you also receive it too. Wonderful I thought so off I went and discovered something that has changed my life. Never could have imagined I would start a practice around it. Here I am today being the facilitator for many people's journey into higher learning and rediscovering their higher selves.

I discovered a true gift and a strong passion simply because I became self-aware, curious, and open. The "disconnected" me would not have noticed how many times the word Reiki came to me. It wouldn't have been curious to learn more, and I wouldn't have been open to trying something new. I am so grateful every day that I am able to do all of this as Reiki has been a true blessing in my life. Now, I can use my expertise in this field of human potential to facilitate Higher Self Breakthroughs with my clients using ancient energy modalities and some of the world's top mind / body techniques which helps my clients move from ordinary to extraordinary in their lives.

Reiki has taught me so much and has absolutely guided me back and helped me reconnect with my higher self. Learning and living the Reiki principles has been wonderful for me. Understanding that everything is energy (I will talk about this in more depth soon).

Below I list the Reiki principles and I invite you to copy them down, place them somewhere you see every day (your mirror, on your desk, on your fridge) and read them every day for 30 days. Consider the possibilities of a new way of being, simply by choosing one principle and living it for one day. Your life will never be the same. Here are the Reiki principles:

- *Just for today, I will not anger (or I will act with love)*
- *Just for today, I will not worry (or I will be peaceful)*
- *Just for today, I will be grateful for all my blessings*
- *Just for today, I will do my work with honesty & integrity*

- *Just for today, I will be kind to all living beings*

Wouldn't you agree these are powerful and yet very simple principles? Just for today…

Growing up, I was never into anything related to science. As an adult, I started to study energy, quantum physics, linguistics, spirituality (among other things) and began to realize how interconnected all these things are. Everything is energy. We have the power to create whatever it is we desire in our lives. We have been gifted with higher faculties to create and manifest all our desires.

The issue is that we have been taught to perceive the world through our 5 senses (sight, sound, taste, smell, touch). As I became more educated, I began to understand that we are quantum and are able to create our future a moment at a time. This is why I love these Reiki principles because it is just one moment in time, just for today. And just for this one moment will eventually turn into just for today which will lead to just for this one week until we eventually get to just for this one life.

We stand at the forefront of massive changes happening now. This is a role encoded within our very own DNA. Each of our paths leading up to now, including earlier this life and past lives, has led to this role. We are Divine Change makers. We are Beacons of the Light. We chose to be here, to experience all these experiences to grow into our greatest and highest good, demonstrating to others they can do it too. This is so beautiful. This is why I have taken on writing this book. It is my way of facing my own fears, pushing my limits, showing you, it can be done so that you can do it too!!!

Each time you become more whole and more loving, you help humanity as a whole and raise consciousness across the planet. Do not underestimate the power of this. When you see injustices and lies, remember your role. Do the best you can to embody justice and truth sourced from love. This is how powerful you and I are. Every time you do for yourself, you are doing for others.

For healing and transformational change, issues must be brought to light and seen for what they are. Do what you can to stay neutral as you process social media discussions and the news. There is a lot of fear in the air - it must be brought to light in order to change the status quo. Inherent to the human condition is a learned fear-based response to the unknown and "outsiders." This is nothing new of course. What's different now is the cumulative effect of raised awareness and the numbers of people who are connected in real time to what's happening globally.

Fear-based labeling of people, religions, and countries must be avoided if we are to have a peaceful world. That's not always easy, even for those on the path of awakening - the fear and DNA-level prejudicial conditioning is that strong. Everyone has it. Therefore, be watchful of your reactions when you hear about refugees settling into your city or construction of a place of worship nearby involving a faith different from yours. We are all one and avoid at all costs judging someone for who they are, for they are one with you.

Recently, my home country Canada, became the leader in Divine Change makers. We welcomed the first Syrian refugees to our country. I have been very moved by this. On Thursday December 10th, 2015 the first group arrived. I experienced very STRONG feelings of gratitude and love coming from individuals I haven't met yet. Many people were fearful of "terrorists" entering the country, yet I was not. I chose not to engage in those thought processes, despite it being something real to consider. I choose to have faith and trust in the entire process and avoid labelling, simply just loving them instead. I want to share with you what our Prime Minster said. Whether you are Canadian or not, read this quote, it resonates in my heart. Justin Trudeau said the following:

"This is something that we are able to do in this country because we define a Canadian not by a skin color or a language or a religion or a background, but by a shared set of values, aspirations, hopes and dreams that people around the world share. And how you will receive these people tonight will be something they will remember for the rest of their lives, but also, I know something that you will remember for the rest of your lives. And I thank you deeply for being a part of this because this matters, tonight matters, not just for Canada but for the world."

Isn't this beautiful? This is something for the world! Just as I mentioned, when you grow as a person, when you step into LOVE, when you choose to live your life at cause rather than effect, this is something you do for the entire world! It is not selfish of you to put yourself first, it allows others to see the possibilities for themselves and know that they can do it too. This is what Canada has, and I am proud to be a part of this.

Disclaimer: Strive to be more discerning. Be your own

truth watchdog. Everything I share here is my own truth, it doesn't have to be yours. Question your questions. Do this for increased discernment and clarification. Example: when something rings true for you and you have received an inner validation that seems to validate that truth, make it your truth and then ask more questions.

No matter how much darkness you encounter, the light is always there. Invite a connection with that light daily, within yourself and within others. Trust that you never walk alone. Spirit is always with you. I love you.

Cleansing Prayer

I AM now choosing to cleanse myself and release any and all thought forms, beings, situations and energies that are no longer of service to my highest and greatest good... across all planes of my existence, across all universes, and across all lifetimes. I ask that all energies that are less than love be transmuted for the highest good of all. And so it is.

CHAPTER 5

Lean In

"The Truth will set you free, but first it will piss you off"
– Gloria Steinem

One day you wake up and realize how far you have come. The dust has settled, the smoke has risen and suddenly you are standing before beautiful rays of sunshine in your life and it feels like a lifetime ago you were stuck in your rut. You are stronger, you are wiser, you are more authentically you and totally okay that some people no longer resonate with you. Evolution and growth in life causes us to see clearly on what it is we want in our lives. All the relationships, friendships, business deals that didn't work out has taught us what we don't want in our lives and allows us to see for the first time glimpses into what we do want.

It is important to focus on what you want. Why? Because focus determines our behaviors and our behaviors determine our results. If we avoid doing this, we give up by default because trust me, the universe will make the choice for you.

Can you think of a time in your life when you felt like the pain would never end? There was zero possibility of the end in sight and you couldn't be convinced otherwise? Then suddenly, almost out of nowhere, you get an opportunity to make a new connection by 'chance'. Perhaps some weird coincidence happened, and you were in the right place at the right time and everything changed. Let me share with you a secret...

THERE IS NO SUCH THING AS CONICIDENCES IN LIFE.

> Period. Everything happens for a reason, exactly as it should, all in support of your greatest and highest good.

People show up to teach us about ourselves. Things fall apart to make room for better things to appear. These pivotal life moments, when everything seems to have gone wrong and we are face to face with our biggest fears, are the moments that define who we are. Will we push through and triumph? Or will we retreat and surrender to defeat?

Everything is happening for us to uncover the areas of our life that need love more. The person you despise the most in life is there teaching you how to love yourself even more. How you may ask? Simple. Everyone is a direct mirror reflection of ourselves. The things we love most (and least) about the people we come in contact with, whether it is our family or a stranger in the grocery store, are bringing into your conscious awareness the areas in your life that is lacking in love. This was a hard one for me to really grasp, and when I did, all my experiences changed to life lessons in self-reflection.

I invite you to try this exercise below. Grab a separate piece of paper and create this chart below. *(This is an exercise Gina Mollicone-Long taught me, and you can learn more about it in her book "Think or Sink".)*

People That Push my Negative Buttons (i.e. DISLIKE)

Name	Qualities I Dislike

People That Push my Positive Buttons (i.e. ADMIRE)

Name	Qualities I Dislike

IN THE MIRROR...

I FORGIVE MYSELF FOR BEING (INSERT QUALITIES FROM NEGATIVE BUTTONS)

_____

_____

_____

I ACKNOWLEDGE MYSELF FOR BEING (INSERT QUALITIES FROM POSITIVE BUTTONS)

_____

_____

_____

All behaviors have a higher positive purpose they are fulfilling. It may not appear that way when someone is coldhearted, lacks empathy, is abusive, however, there is always a higher purpose. That person is just lacking the resources available to assist them in getting their needs met in a healthier way. Needs are non-negotiable. Reflect on the chart you just created and ask yourself "what is the need that this person is attempting to have met by the behavior they are displaying?" Brainstorm the positive intention with the negative behavior and you will see how a person who lacks empathy simply does not realize they have the tools to be more empathic in that moment.

This idea, that all behaviors are positive, and just lack resources, allows us to separate intention from the behavior. You are not your behaviors. You are perfect and perhaps all that is needed is a shift in perception to see that. This is an empowered place to stand in for ourselves, and for other people.

CHAPTER 6

Believe in Better Days

"The Secret to Living is Giving"
– Anthony Robbins

Our Emotions are trying to get our attention, but we keep ignoring and resisting them. Sometimes, pain arises to get our attention, we ignore that too. Then suddenly, the wizard of Oz house falls on our head and finally we get the wake up call we needed. Avoid having the house fall on your head. Pay attention in the now. What is going on? What are you experiencing? Is it serving your highest good? If not, why not?

Think of emotions as a child that only wants your love. They are trying to get your attention until you finally face them and accept them for what they are - emotions. They are not YOUR emotions, they are just feelings in the body that we tie a story to and it is actually healthy to feel all emotions, we are human after all. Be happy ALL the time is actually unhealthy. Feeling the full range of emotions is healthy. The key is when we are in the lower vibrational energy, to move from this as quickly as possible and avoid spinning in that story. Resource and get out.

Sometimes it can feel like the negative emotions are taking over – my message to you is ALWAYS BELIEVE IN BETTER DAYS. Negative emotions will not last forever. You may be going through the toughest challenges of your life right now. Perhaps you are in a Dark Night moment and faced with a life-threatening diagnosis, or maybe a divorce, or perhaps you have lost your job. Trust me when I say this, better days are ahead and this mess you are in right now will become your message to share with others. You will overcome whatever it is you are going through, you will rise to the top and you will be able to support others faced with similar challenges. I believe all our challenges make us teachers. It is our duty to pass the torch and guide others who need us now.

Since all we have is NOW, you won't get out of the Dark Night tomorrow, you will only get out of it NOW! The key to getting out of it is LOVING - the only reason we are on Earth. Like our egos, the Dark Night is just an illusion. We have always been HOME and have been the LIGHT the whole time while looking for it in the Dark Night. Of course, we have been the LIGHT, how else would we have been aware of the dark? If we were dark too, we wouldn't be able to observe the dark, wouldn't you agree?

As I write to you now, on Christmas Eve 2015, I am choosing to love in the now because for the past few hours, I was choosing to "do" depression. I went to church with the family, enjoyed watching the kids be a part of the play, and as soon as I got home, my mood changed, and I chose to stay stuck in it for a while. We always have a choice, and we are human, so emotion is healthy and normal. The moment I chose to sit up straight, utilize an outlet (this book) and work through the blah blah blah story I was telling myself (which was creating those emotions), I immediately started feeling better... interesting, isn't it?

Take this beautiful time to face and embrace the dark once and for all. Let the light of LOVE shine on it and dissolve it. You are awakened NOW. You are LOVE NOW. There is no other way it could be. Anything else is merely a dream! The more you resist the Dark Night or the "stuck" place you are in, the more you keep repeating the lessons you need to learn. Accept and embrace where you are NOW. Embrace this pain and suffering.

Know that you are helpless in this process and the key is to surrender to LOVE. Use your pain as the catalyst for a great transformation and rebirth. Any transformation in life has got to go through some pain right before. Birth is most painful right before coming out of the birth canal. Caterpillars, snakes, and crabs go through a transformation where the old self "dies" to the new self. Be like the phoenix and rise above the ashes of your old false self just by being the LOVE that you are! Life is all about cycles. NOTHING lasts forever. View this process as a rite of passage for a remarkable rebirth. You will finally be free from the baggage you have clung onto for so long through resistance.

CHAPTER 7

You've Got The Power

"Knowing yourself is the beginning to all wisdom."
- Aristotle

When I began to experience and understand the power that lies within, I made it my life's mission to share and teach it to as many people as I can. Knowing that everything that has ever happened in this life, and past lives, has been stored in my unconscious mind, I started to speak differently. I was able to see the world with fresh eyes, my awakening has happened, and I now wish to share this knowledge with all in this world.

What's really cool is that in order for us to consciously have an experience of something, our unconscious mind needs to filter all that information in a manageable way in order for us to experience what we call reality.

There is a Harvard study, referred by many as "*The Magic Number 7*", which outlines just exactly how information is processed and how our conscious mind can only manage 7 ± two "chunks" of information at a time. This applies to anything and everything. Ask any marketing guru and they will agree with this as it has been proven most people cannot remember more than 7 brands of a similar product at one time. Try it for yourself right now. Name 7 white wines from Italy. If wine isn't your thing, name 7 car manufactures that have Hybrid vehicles. Try it. Go on…

How many did you get? 7? Maybe 5? Interesting isn't it?

This study led me to others where I found how powerful our unconscious mind is, and while this may sound cliché, yet in a moment I am sure you will be able to see what I mean.

While your unconscious mind is able to absorb and store everything that is happening around you, estimated at a whopping 2,000,000 bits per second of information (some would argue now that number is closer to 8 - 10,000,000 bits per second), your conscious mind can only handle about 7± 2 "chunks," or roughly 134 bits per second. That is A LOT of processing that gets done moment to moment. I often ask people to imagine if they had to *consciously* focus on breathing, some of us would be dead within two minutes. This is what our unconscious mind is for. Not only does the unconscious mind run the body, it also stores all memories, organizes all memories (using the gestalt), it keeps you safe and truly desires to serve you – it just needs SUPER clear instructions to do so.

In order for us to have a conscious experience of the world – what we call an "Internal Representation" in NLP, or the movie in your mind – our unconscious mind has to "filter" the 2,000,000 bits of information down to 134 manageable bits, each second. It filters the information in three ways: It will *delete, distort, and generalize* those 2,000,000 bits and it does that based on the following filters that run deep in your mind.

- Your environment (Time, Space, Matter and Energy)
- Language
- Memories
- Decisions

- Meta-Programs
- Attitudes
- Beliefs
- Values

Many of these filters are largely or entirely unconscious and when my clients need new tools, I use the tools of NLP to change them rapidly and easily.

What we are left with is our Internal Representation or our *conscious experience*. Couple that together with your Physiology, and this gives you your current State.

All of our behavior and results are based on our State. Why is that? Well, because when our body feels good, and our internal representation is clean and positive, this gives us the push to take action on the things we want to accomplish. When our body and internal representation doesn't feel good, we will resist doing the things we have to do in order to get the results we want.

We are creatures of habit and often desire the road that is most comfortable, which really leads us to where we do not want to go. For example, when you are sick, you rather do nothing but stay in bed because your body doesn't feel well plus pair this with the movie in your mind of "I am sick right now" and in turn your state will produce those results. If instead we acknowledge that our body is showing symptoms of something to get our attention (because this is all it ever does) and we keep our internal representation focused on being healthy, these results will be produced.

Do this the next time your body is showing symptoms of a flu or cold. Before you go to sleep at night, TELL your unconscious mind that as you sleep you would like it to increase your immune system, so these symptoms will eliminate themselves. Tell your unconscious mind. It is not to ask it, order and command it. Feel free to add in … that you will wake up feeling rested and energized or anything else you would like it to do for you. This works. I used this technique a few weeks ago when I felt a cold coming on. Each night before bed, I would instruct my unconscious mind to increase my immune system and after two nights the symptoms were completely gone.

Our bodies will tell us what we need to know. A body filled with disease is simply a body not at ease (dis-ease) and any physical pain you are experiencing is simply getting you to *pay attention in the now*.

Recently, I had a client who was suffering from chronic back pain. She was doing everything she could to release these symptoms, but the pain would still be there. 15 minutes on a Skype call, she went from a 9/10 on the pain scale to 0!!! All we did was have her acknowledge what emotions she was experiencing in that moment.

Focus is key. Going back to the book's introduction, when we focus on what we want, our unconscious mind cannot tell if it is really happening or just imagined and it will work with you to create this in your reality. This is why we must guard our thoughts so closely and always ensure they are focused towards our desired outcomes and not on what we do not want.

Now the question is, what do you really want for your life? What kind of legacy do you want to leave? What type of experiences do you want to create for yourself? The choice is all yours. Imagine the life you desire. Write it all down and feeeeeeeel the feelings you will have once it is accomplished. Act as if you already have it (by feeling the feelings of it) and go out there and take action daily towards the accomplishment of your goals. Be fearless and fierce with your actions. Stubbornly focus on what you want and never ever give up on yourself or your dreams. You have everything that it takes already inside of you, tap in and unleash that NOW. You got this.

CHAPTER 8

Creating Heaven on Earth: 55 things to live better days, now!

"The best and most beautiful things in the world cannot be seen or even touched - they must be felt with the heart."
Helen Keller

Often times, "where do I begin?" is the question I am asked most. My answer is always, "Where are you now?" You see, we have to know where we are and where we want to go in order to get to where we should be. So, ask yourself: "Where am I now?" What have you done in the past to get the results you want? What do you need to do more of each day? It is in the little things day to day that make the difference. Sure, taking the big jump and going all in is an option as well, but why not just take it one step at a time. Like my dear friend James MacNeil says: "Just be brave enough to take the NEXT step." That's all you ever need to do.

So, what do you need to do? Make a list of all the things that you need to do in order to get closer to your goal. Also make a list of all the things you don't want to do that you MUST in order to achieve your goal and start checking them off one by one. It will feel so good once completed.

Here is a list of things to do to make your life a better version of itself. You can also email melissa@betterdaysnow.ca for a copy.

1. **Daily Gratitude:** Each morning write 3-5 things down on paper of what you are grateful for. Feel the emotions of gratitude run through your body. Gratitude is the gateway to abundance. When you are grateful for what you currently have, it makes room for more to come in.

2. **Smile at Strangers:** You never know what someone is going through, why not share your gift of a smile to make someone's day? It is free to give

and may be the only good thing that happens to them that day.

3. **Set intentions before you eat:** Take a moment to pause before you eat your meal. Give thanks for the food, all the people who prepared it and feel all the nourishments, taste all the flavors, indulge all your senses. When we set positive intentions with our food, we become healthier and food tastes so much better too.

4. **Move your body:** We are energy, and energy prefers to be in motion. Exercise and movement is fundamental to your well BEing. Get out and have fun, dance, twirl, walk, play.

5. **Epson Salt Baths:** One of my favorite things to do. This is a very spiritual grounding activity. Light a candle, get some oils, pour in the Epson salts and relax your mind and body away. The fluidity of the water allows for heightened meditation and clear ideas to come through.

6. **Read Thought Provoking Books:** Reading keeps the mind active and alive. We get the opportunity to learn from some of the great's by reading their

books. We can expand our awareness by choosing material that inspires us to take action.

7. **Colour:** The big new trend now is the adult colouring books, I must admit, I like it too. This is a form of meditation, creation, relaxation and what I love the most about it is that it allows for your childlike self to come through.

8. **Walk in nature:** If you want peace in your life, go for a walk in nature is the best way to start. Feeling the energy of the earth, listening to all the sounds, observing everything you see, and noticing how everything blends into each other is so peaceful, grounding, exhilarating and peaceful. Want to take it a step further? Walk barefoot on the ground for an instant shift into a more centered and grounded BEing.

9. **Learn a new skill or hobby:** What is one thing you always wanted to learn? Perhaps a new language, or maybe archery, why not pottery? Each year challenge yourself to learn something new. This will keep your brain young and your mind free.

10. **Drink Room Temperature Water:** Research has shown that drinking cold water shocks your sys-

tem and it is recommended to drink water at room temperature instead. If you want to go above and beyond, why not invest in an alkaline water system to ensure that your PH levels are where they need to be. When we are too acidic (which most of us are) this is when we are at higher risk for cancers and other forms of disease (when our body is not at ease it creates dis-ease). When we drink alkalinized water, it allows our body to be in a natural alkaline state where disease (dis-ease) cannot grow.

11. **Avoid consuming negative content (ie. news):** Mainstream news is meant to perpetuate fear within us. I prefer to use alternative new sources (thank you internet) and yet I still encourage you to check and research stories for factual information. Information is so readily available to us now, choose wisely what you consume. If you do consume mainstream news, avoid doing it right before bed.

12. **Play with an animal:** Animals are so wonderful as they always demonstrate love. Pet a cat for 15 minutes or play with a dog to lower your blood

pressure and stress levels. It also is a great way to allow your childlike self to shine through and have some fun.

13. **Dance in the Rain:** This is so MAGICAL! If you haven't done this before, DO IT!! The rain is cleansing, and again, brings out the child in us.

14. **Write a book:** You have a story to tell. It is such a rewarding (and vulnerable) experience to write all your thoughts for the world to read. Whether you decide to publish your book or not is up to you. I say write it, be you and share your gifts with the world.

15. **Forgive someone:** Forgiveness is for self, not for the other person. We all hold onto stuff for years and that only brews disease, negativity and hatred in your life. Avoid doing this. Forgiveness will truly set you free. Get a pen and paper and write it all out. Forgive someone that you would like to release from your day to day thoughts. Dispose of the letter safely afterwards by burning it, flushing it down the toilet, shredding it etc. This is a process that can be done silently. If you need to ask for forgiveness, see below.

16. **Forgive yourself:** Ask for forgiveness for something you have done, write the letter, be brave, and give the person a call. You will feel so much better and they will respect and honor you for your bravery. We all co-create each situation in life, take responsibility for your part in it.

17. **Avoid eating processed food and meats:** Eat foods that are as close as possible to their natural state. Raw, organic, colourful foods are so delicious and it gives our body the natural elements needed to function and operate in a peak state. When we reduce our meat consumption, not only will your body thank you, the planet will too. Did you know that vegetarians and vegans have a smaller carbon footprint too? Why not do your part for yourself and the planet?

18. **Say I love you:** Every day, at least once a day, stand in front of the mirror and say I Love You – out loud. How often do we say I love you to ourselves or other people? Take time each day to say it to yourself and you will notice how you will want to say it to other people. Encourage people to do this as well. Remind people how proud of

them you are. Meaningful words will sing in our souls forever.

19. **Volunteer once a month:** When you GIVE you GET. Volunteer one hour a month to a cause that you are passionate about. Perhaps you can go to the animal shelter and play with the dogs, maybe you can go to your local homeless shelter and prepare meals, or perhaps you have a gift or skill that you can donate to the community.

20. **Star gaze:** On a clear night in the city or go for a drive into the country. Connect with the universe by gazing at the stars. Acknowledge the infinite amount of possibilities and realize you are here right now.

21. **Travel by yourself:** Go on at least one solo trip in your life. I did mine on my 30th birthday and it was great. No schedules to check, no permission needed, just go and explore.

22. **Use the good sheets and fine china:** Why not put the all white sheets on and use the fine china for spaghetti night? Often, we 'wait' for a special occasion to use these things, why not use them now? Today is special. You are special. Use the

good sheets and fine china.

23. **Get out of your comfort zone:** Nothing fun ever happens in the comfort zone. Why not push yourself to do one thing that scares you every day? You will reap the rewards of bravery.

24. **Meditate:** Spend some time alone with your thoughts in reflection and prayer. Meditation can be as simple as walking in nature or staring at a flame. It is in silence we are able to receive the messages from the Divine.

25. **Journal:** This is a great way to keep track of your experiences and reflect on them often. It is also a great way to manifest intentions, get your thoughts on paper, release things that are bothering you, and so much more.

26. **Learn more about crystals:** Crystals are natural elements from the earth that carry strong energetic properties and intentions. I love learning about different crystals and their meanings. I have many in my space that assist me in balancing my energy, grounding myself, and amplifying what already exists within.

27. Smudge yourself and your space: Burning sage, or smudging, is part of my day to day routine. This is an ancient indigenous ritual that dates back thousands of years and is used by many today. It aids in grounding and clearing you and your space. You will notice shifts in how the space feels after smudging. Cleanse yourself by allowing the smoke to surround your body and then walk around your space going into each corner using positive intentions to remove the negative or stuck energy.

28. Laugh every day: Laughter truly is the best medicine. Find as many ways possible to laugh on a daily basis, especially on the days you do not feel like laughing.

29. Develop an endless curiosity with this world: Curiosity is one of the best gifts you can give your life. Be curious about all the possibilities, all the opportunities, all the challenges. Find creative ways to discover new things about yourself and life.

30. Remember people's names: This is such a simple and meaningful thing to do. Whether it is a person you have just been introduced to, or the cashier where you are shopping. Say their name in your head when you first hear it (or read it on their name tag), and then repeat it out loud. Greet people as if you know them.

31. **Learn to focus only on the present:** Avoid worrying about the future or being stuck in the past. All we have is right now. You either live in the now or, in essence, you are not living at all.

32. **Even more specifically, live in THIS moment:** This begins with your breath. Focus on what is happening around you. Be aware. Even with this book you are holding right now (either in book or ebook form, you can still do this exercise). Take a moment, smell the scent of the paper, feel the sensations and textures of the book in your hands, hear the sounds of the pages turning, see the colours. Be present and just breathe.

33. **Avoid taking life so seriously:** Life is meant to be lived in a joyful and fun way. Avoid taking life so seriously. Always seek satisfaction and fun in your day to day. Be childlike in your behaviors and thoughts. Enjoy life to the fullest.

34. Get in the sun: The sun will rejuvenate your spirit and energy. Gently gaze at the sun when it is early in the morning (avoid doing so at its peak). Take your sunglasses off sometimes and let the sun beam through you.

35. Help others: When you give, you get. Plain and simple. Help people whenever possible. If it means giving someone a boost, picking something up that fell, or giving someone a cup of coffee in the drive thru behind you. Be generous with what you have. Always have Time and a Smile to give.

36. Be the person to make others feel special: Always raise people up. Tell someone that you are proud of them. Say thank you to a stranger for opening a door for you. Lift someone's spirit who is having a bad day. Be everyone's cheerleader.

37. Visualize daily: Our imagination is one of our higher faculties, why not use it to get the things we want? Now, let's be clear, seeing yourself accomplishing your goal does not mean it will manifest with a strong desire for it and massive action towards its attainment. This is always required along with this powerful technique.

38. **Use Essential Oils:** I recently started to learn about the wonderful health and spiritual benefits of essential oils. They are very powerful and can really enhance your focus, relaxation, ease some physical symptoms, and so much more. I enjoy using them in my bath or defusing them to have the whole room smelling of the scent you choose. Be sure to use good quality oils and use them safely. Email melissa@betterdaysnow.ca if you would like a recommendation on a top-quality brand I believe is best to use.

39. **Learn a new language (or sign language):** If we are not growing we are dying. Why not learn something new and grow your mind in ways that will expand your skill sets, bring more pleasure into your life, and be a really cool conversation starter at a dinner party or social event.

40. **Garden:** Using our hands, especially when touching the earth, is very therapeutic. It allows you to feel more grounded and connected to the earth. It is also a beautiful metaphor on how planting seeds and being patient in the process of growth

can be a beautiful and rewarding thing.

41. **Come up with a life mantra:** What would yours be? Sometimes when people ask me "How's it going?" I like to answer, "Living the dream – one day at a time". This usually gets a laugh or two. Or how about "Everything is working out in my favor". One of my Dad's favorite responses is "Top shelf or Top drawer with top shelf being higher." A mantra is a firm belief in something that you repeat over and over to yourself.

42. **Celebrate one success every day:** This is an important element to further your personal and career success, celebrating it! So why not take it and celebrate one thing every day that you successfully accomplished. Not only will this allow you to be even more grateful, it will also allow you the opportunity to see how far you have come. Celebrate one win each and every day.

43. **Create a bucket list and start checking them off:** This is such a fun activity. I recently attended a bucket list party my friend Carol hosted, and this was so eye opening as to all the things we want to do in life, and how often we just don't think we

can do it. Why not live life with a bunch of "Oh well's" as opposed to "what if?"

44. **Learn to give Heart to Heart hugs:** I am constantly practicing this with every person I hug. A heart to heart hug is when you lean in with your left side (as does the other person) so your hearts connect. For whatever reason, we have been so unconsciously programmed to hug the other way, yet when I show people this, their eyes light up. Go for it, hug heart to heart and feel the connection.

45. **Practice heart breathing:** HeartMath is an institute that I was introduced to by my teacher and trainer Gina Mollicone-Long. They have conducted extensive research around the heart and the energetic frequencies it puts out. Heart breathing is taught by visualizing that your breath is coming from your heart and expanding with each breath. Try it and feel the difference.

46. **Pick up every coin you find and bless it:** Some say coins are signs angels are nearby. I like to believe that, and I also believe that it is abundance flowing in. Every coin you find, pick it up and say

thank you and put it in your piggy bank. You were meant to find it at that moment. Tap into the cosmic synergies that happen all around you, give thanks and send love to the universe.

47. **Write thank you on the back of each cheque you deposit or send out:** This has been so profound for me. I started to write on the back of my cheques "I am abundant, thank you" and man does this ever work! Also, with each bill payment you make, say thank you and give thanks that you are able to pay it now, even if it is just the minimum payment, you will see how important this task is once you are consistent with it.

48. **Talk to people you do not know:** One of the greatest joy's in life is being acknowledged by a stranger. Say hello as you pass by them on the street. Make eye contact and smile. Give out compliments to people, make them feel good.

49. **Train yourself to enjoy something you don't currently like:** I used to always say "I don't like sushi". Well guess what, now I do. I trained myself, and honestly, I simply accepted an invitation to go out one day and discovered something com-

pletely new that I really enjoy. Life is meant to be this way. Live a little, enjoy the sushi, try the new fruit that looks weird, and why not just go for it?

50. **Wish your mom a happy "Birth Giving Day" on your birthday:** Or if your mom is no longer with us, consider this for other people you know who have children. It is the mom who did all the hard work on the day of your birth, and yes, it is a celebration for you of course. Why not take it to an even deeper level and acknowledge the person who gave life to you on that day, trust me, it will move mountains.

51. **Accept others for who they are – parents and children too:** It is so true that we are all doing the best we can with what we have. Accept people, flaws and all, as perfect and miraculous beings of life. Lead by example so others know it is safe for them too, and in their own time, this will leave new resources and skills to allow them to reveal their greatness.

52. **Connect with water whenever possible:** Water is very calming, naturally healing, and can be a very spiritual experience. Whenever possible, go

to the lake, an ocean, or even a river. Be still and watch the fluidity of the water moving. Listen to the sounds, smell all the delicious smells. Water is abundantly available to use, and it allows for amazing insight to pour through.

53. **Bless those who are bothering you:** This is a powerful exercise that Bob Proctor taught me. Whenever there is someone bothering you, instead of feeding into the negative emotions of it all, why not send them love? Each morning for about 2-3 minutes, focus on sending them love. Visualize a beam of light coming from you and reaching them. Truly feeeeeeeeel love for them. It may be a challenge yet will yield great results.

54. **Tell a friend you are proud of them:** Sometimes we forgot our friends need support and kind words too. Perhaps you have a friend who is going through the usual up's and down's, why not send a text and say, "I am proud of you". Or perhaps this can be your child who is working hard on making friends or on an assignment and would really lift them up. Our words are some of the most powerful gifts we have, why not share them now?

55. Buy food for a homeless person: This is a kind gesture that will go a long way. Take them into the store with you and let them decide what they want. Or maybe surprise them and take a moment to chat and find out their story. Show them love, they need it.

CHAPTER 9

Self-Awareness is Key!

"Self-Awareness at its finest is accepting your short comings and accentuating your strengths"
Gary Vaynerchuck

Let's put all this together for you in this final chapter. We have embarked on a miraculous journey of self-discovery and personal power in this book. You are now equipped with some great tools and resources to start you off on this journey. We have discovered that our focus, language and thought processes are very important. We acknowledge and accept that we will have the lows in life because this is what allows us to learn, grow and more importantly, appreciate the highs in life. We have talked about some ideas to help us in our day to day, and if I were to sum it up in one sentence what this all means is simply:

Self-Awareness is Key!

Self-awareness can be defined as "conscious knowledge of one's own character, feelings, motives, and desires."

This is how we tap in. Listening to our bodies, focusing on what we want, acknowledging the language we use and correcting it when it is not geared towards our desires.

Everything that shows up in your life is to bring you into alignment with your higher self and this is done through self-awareness. This is how we begin to create heaven on earth. By listening and honouring ourselves and what makes sense in your model of the world. We all experience life and "reality" in our own unique way. We can have similar experiences, but no two are the same because, as outline in chapter 5, we all have different perceptions of reality based on deep unconscious programming running in our unconscious mind.

Failure is nothing more than feedback. Edison said it best when he was working on creating the lightbulb. He said "I have not *failed*. I've just found 10,000 ways that won't work." Edison was self-aware. He took what didn't work and instead of beating himself up for it, he used it as feedback to do something different on the next try.

Success, in any area of life, is mainly dependent on your outlook and mindset. Self-awareness is the key to that.

One of the greatest entrepreneurs of this century is Mr. Gary Vaynerchuck who talks in depth about the importance of self-awareness in life and business. He says openly that he knows he sucks at a lot of things, and where he is winning is in his ability to be self-aware enough to know this. He will not pretend he is good at something, not at all, and neither should you. Bet on your strengths, go all in on them and avoid thinking you have to be great at everything. Self-awareness requires understanding your strengths and focusing on those while acknowledging your short comings and making the CHOICE to work with what you have going for you.

How can you become more self-aware? Firstly, take inventory of yourself. What are your strengths, what are you really good at? What are some of your short comings? I will give you an example. One of my strengths is excellent communication skills. Aside from being a Gemini, which governs communication, I have worked and studied communication for many years – this is a strength. One of my shortcomings is my spelling and grammar are subpar. I knew when writing this book, I would be able to story tell and communicate well with you and I was going to need a strong editor to assist me with the punctuation. This is what I got, someone whose strengths are in grammar and spelling (thanks Dad for being my great editor). I delegated, plain and simple.

So, what are your strengths? Take inventory of the things you are really good at and the things you really enjoy doing. Make a list so you can see it in front of you. Then, make a list of the things you are not so good at and have no desire to improve. Do this inventory check frequently. In the book "Think and Grow Rich" it is discussed that every year you should do a year-end review. What did you accomplish, what did you learn, this will allow you a clear analysis of your results that you did or did not achieve and will keep you on track to your goals.

How can you make yourself better? It is not about being better than others, which is a dangerous game to play, it is about being better than the person you were yesterday. In life, if we are not growing we are dying so may you forever be challenged to grow and change. May you always find opportunities to discover new things about yourself, and may you always be a beacon of the light demonstrating to others that it is safe for them to do so too.

You see, when we stand in our power, when we speak our truth, when we live our life authentically and openly, this unconsciously allows others to do the same as well. Be the light, shine it bright to touch the lives of every person you come in contact with. If you, just you, do this, the world will transform into a better place. As Mahatma Gandhi says, "Be the change you want to see in the world" and as I have discovered, when you are the change in your world, everything around you starts to change, and other people's world's will change as well. We will all one day be living heaven here on earth as we will be living in alignment, living in love shining our light so others will feel safe to do the same as well.

In closing, all I wish to say to you is: Choose Love. Choose to be it, choose to share it, choose to receive it. The world is changing right before our eyes, and despite mass chaos, the inhumane actions that are occurring all over the world, this I know for sure.... When we choose love, when we choose the light, the darkness cannot exist for long. Right now, darkness is running rampant in our world; whether it is overseas with wars or the wars in our own backyard.

Love will always win for it is the only thing that truly exists, everything else is just an illusion.

It all begins with you. Will you choose to love yourself? What would this feel like for you? What would be the words you would speak to those who are listening if you had just one chance right now? How would your life look if you choose to live in love?

What has happened in the past is done. You have become the person you are today because of all those experiences. Cherish that. The world needs you, and that chaotic mess you once lived in can serve purpose to many people if you turn that mess into your message.

Be the change. Choose love. The world needs you right now.

"My closing thoughts:

Write a letter to your younger self. Share your experiences on the pages to follow of all the things you are grateful to have learned and experienced and what it has taught you about yourself.

What advice would you give your younger self today knowing all the things you know now? Write it out below and remind yourself frequently.

Here is a piece of what I wrote to the younger Me:

Dear Younger Me,

I just want you to know...

I love you. I think you are so beautiful and so wonderful to be around. People feel good when they are with you and that is a wonderful gift to have.

*I want you to know everything is going to be alright. Put your faith in the Lord and believe that **better days** are ahead. The plan for your life is way bigger than you can imagine and all the things you are experiencing now are simply preparing you for what is to come. You got this!*

There will be times when you will doubt yourself, when you will want to give up, when you will feel life is pointless and you will want to go home, don't. This world needs you. Your light is so bright and will touch many lives. You are going to do incredible things in your life and will meet tremendous people, learn from them.

Give 100% in everything you do, every conversation you have, every moment you get – it will pay off. I am so proud of you and I want you to know that what lies ahead for you is something so miraculous that it will seem like your life is a movie, and in theory, it kinda is.

Never give up and always go for it. I love you, I am proud of you, and thank you for being you.

With Love and Gratitude,

Your 33 year old self

> Now it is your turn. Get some more paper if you would like to go real deep.

Dear Younger Me,

I just want you to know…

Since the writing of this book...

Vulnerability Alert

Full disclosure, OMG, did I ever prolong this process. Thank you to everyone who waited so patiently for me to get this done. Thank you to everyone who encouraged me to complete this. Nearly two years since writing this book, I am finally getting it out.

Everything you have read in this book has come straight from my heart, I hope you felt that turning each page. I had so much fear creep in that it crippled me, and I was living at effect to this for a long time. Wow, that feels better to say publicly now.

This is an immensely personal story I put into paper. I didn't even know I had this fear until one thing after another happened in post-production that caused a few setbacks, which eventually allowed me to become my own set back. But here it is, and I hope you loved it.

Part of my hesitation also was I was embarrassed. I wrote all these wonderful things, and then I got trapped by it. Cause and effect... the main theme of this book... and here I was not practicing what I was preaching. This allowed me to feel extremely human, and this is important, because I am.

I also found that my life, my work, had completely transformed since writing this book. I didn't feel connected to it as much anymore. However, this book is for you, not for me, and I know those picking it up to read it will get exactly what they need from it. That makes me feel good and grateful.

Since completing this book, I am now a certified Reiki Master Teacher and Generational Healer ™. I still work with Hypnosis and NLP, yet my calling made its way into energy work. I just love it. My business has grown so much, I have served hundreds of clients now with all of my modalities and taught over 50 students Reiki. My calling runs deep in this work. I am so grateful to be in service. It is an honour I hold close to my heart when someone chooses me to be their guide, and I have been amazed at people's ability to take charge of their lives, be open to healing, and the transformations that occur when we simply lean into love and life. It is so magical.

In March 2016 I had a full circle moment when I was invited to speak on a panel of female entrepreneurs for The United Nations Association of Canada's International Women's Day Forum that was held at The Royal York Hotel. It was so amazing and so surreal to be back in the place that this book was birthed and now being interviewed for the work I do in the community. It was an experience I'll never forget.

Most importantly, since writing this book, I am now a mother to my Queen Makeeba. She was born on November 14th, 2017. I am so honoured to join this sacred calling into motherhood. I have always wanted to be a mother, and I am so honoured she chose me to be her mom. You are the light of my life, thank you for giving me a deeper meaning to life. I look forward to all the adventures that await us. When you were in my womb, we were very connected to sharing this work. There were so many shifts and so much healing that occurred and I am committed more than ever to be a great role model and support to you (hints why I am getting this book out now I'm sure). I love you with every corner of my heart.

February 2018

Thank you. I love you.

About the Author

Melissa Maher offers a holistic approach to transformation utilizing some of the world's TOP MIND / BODY and ENERGY techniques. These techniques include one-on-one NLP Coaching, Time Line Therapy ®, Hypnotherapy and Reiki Energy.

Melissa created **Better Days NOW**, in 2014, a company that is dedicated to empowering women to raise their self-esteem, live balanced lives and discover their limitless human potential. Her passion to help others developed years ago when she experienced the abundance the universe provides when you clean up your past and release all limiting beliefs about what's possible, act daily towards your goals, and stubbornly focus on what you want (she always knew her stubbornness would come in handy one day).

Melissa loves to educate through workshops and seminars and has moved audience's large and small, educating and empowering people across the nation. Her unique abilities rests in her one on one work with clients.

Using NLP and Time Line Therapy ®, techniques, Melissa works to discover the root cause of the negative emotions and limiting beliefs we tell ourselves in order to clean up our past and move forward taking action to receive all of our desires.

Whether it is to increase productivity at work, release some excess weight, or create better relationships, if you are searching for a happier life overall, Melissa is sure to get you results that stick.

For more information visit www.betterdaysnow.ca

www.ingramcontent.com/pod-product-compliance
Lightning Source LLC
Chambersburg PA
CBHW070624300426
44113CB00010B/1654